Motherhood

Motherhood

AN ANTHOLOGY
OF VERSE AND PROSE

SMITHMARK

This edition published in 1994 by
SMITHMARK Publishers Inc.
16 East 32nd Street
New York
NY 10016

SMITHMARK books are available for bulk purchase for
sales promotion and for premium use. For details write or
call the manager of special sales, SMITHMARK Publishers
Inc. 16 East 32nd Street, New York, 10016; (212)
532–6600

ISBN 0 8317 3834 0

Produced by Anness Publishing Limited
1 Boundary Row
London SE1 8HP

Printed and bound by Star Standard, Singapore

Contents

Chapter One

THE DEAR AND TENDER TIE
6

Chapter Two

AND I WILL SING A LULLABY
20

Chapter Three

NEVER MIND BABY, MOTHER IS BY
30

Chapter Four

IT SEEMS TO ME BUT YESTERDAY . . .
46

ACKNOWLEDGEMENTS
64

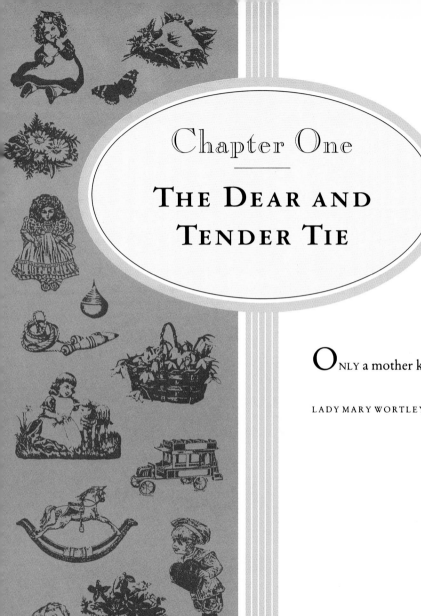

Chapter One

The Dear and Tender Tie

ONLY a mother knows a mother's fondness

LADY MARY WORTLEY MONTAGU, JULY 1754

To my dear little Marianne I shall "dedicate" this book, which, if I should not live to give it her myself, will I trust be reserved for her as a token of her Mother's love and extreme anxiety in the formation of her little daughter's character. If that little daughter should in time become a mother herself, she may take an interest in the experience of another; and at any rate she will perhaps like to become acquainted with her character in its earliest form. I wish that (if ever she sees this) I could give her the slightest idea of the love and the hope that is bound up in her. The love which passeth every earthly love, and the hope that however we may be separated on earth, we may each of us so behave while sojourning here that we may meet again to renew the dear and tender tie of Mother and Daughter.

ELIZABETH GASKELL (1810–1865) FROM HER DIARY

To A W : A Mother

WHEN beside you to your bed
Comes the little catkin-head
(For she surely boasts some fair
Down or beech-leaf colored hair
Your endowing aspects taught her
His and yours, this first-born daughter)
Think how many, blessed two,
Babe and mother, prayed for you.

HELEN PARRY EDEN

From *Coal and Candlelight, and other verses*

Published by the Bodley Head 1918

I begin to love this little creature, and to anticipate [her] birth as a fresh twist to a knot, which I do not wish to untie.

MARY WOLLSTONECRAFT

My Mother

Who fed me from her gentle breast,
And hushed me in her arms to rest,
And on my cheek sweet kisses prest?
  My Mother.

When pain and sickness made me cry,
Who gazed upon my heavy eye,
And wept, for fear that I should die?
  My Mother.

Who dressed my doll in clothes so gay,
And fondly taught me how to play,
And minded all I had to say?
  My Mother.

Who ran to help me when I fell,
And would some pretty story tell,
Or kiss the place to make it well?
  My Mother.

And can I ever cease to be
Affectionate and kind to thee,
Who was so very kind to me,
  My Mother?

ANNE TAYLOR 1782 – 1866

Once in Royal David's City

ONCE in royal David's city
 Stood a lowly cattle shed,
Where a mother laid her baby
 In a manger for his bed:
Mary was that mother mild,
Jesus Christ her little child.

And through all his wondrous childhood,
 He would honour and obey,
Love and watch the lowly maiden
 In whose gentle arms he lay:
Christian children all must be
Mild, obedient, good as he.

CECIL FRANCES ALEXANDER (1818–1895) *Once In Royal David's City*

ON this my beloved little Mossy's birthday I send you a few lines before leaving for Rome. Our little darling will miss us today. She is such a love, such a little sunbeam, so good and so gifted, she will be a charming little person one day, but sometimes I fear not a very happy one, for she is so sensitive and her little heart so tender and warm and loving, so clinging that she is sure to suffer a good deal through life – as those must whose feelings are deep and keen, and who have much love to bestow.

PRINCESS VICTORIA, CROWN PRINCESS OF GERMANY

MARIANNE is now becoming every day more and more interesting. She looks at and tries to take hold of everything. She has pretty good ideas of distance and does not try to catch sunbeams now, as she did two months ago. Her sense of sight is much improved lately in seeing objects at a distance, and distinguishing them. For instance, I had her in my arms to-day in the drawing room, and her Papa was going out of the gate, and she evidently knew him; smiled and kicked. She begins to show a decided preference to those she likes; she put out her little arms to come to me, and would, I am sure, do so to her Papa. She catches the expression of a countenance to which she is accustomed directly; when we laugh, she laughs; and when I look attentive to William's reading, it is quite ridiculous to see her little face of gravity, and earnestness, as if she understood every word. I try always to let her look at anything which attracts her notice as long as she will, and when I see her looking very intently at anything, I take her to it, and let her exercise all her senses upon it, even to tasting, if I am sure it can do her no harm. My object is to give her a habit of fixing her attention.

ELIZABETH GASKELL, from her diary, 1835

The Birthday Present

"Serezha!" she repeated, just above the child's ear.

He raised himself again on his elbow, moved his tousled head from side to side as if seeking for something, and opened his eyes. Silently and questioningly he gazed for a few moments at his mother, who stood motionless before him; then suddenly smiling blissfully, he closed his heavy eyelids and fell once more, not backwards, but forwards into her arms.

"Serezha, my dear little boy!" she uttered, catching her breath and embracing his plump little body.

"Mama!" he muttered, wriggling about in her arms so as to touch them with different parts of his body.

Sleepily smiling with closed eyes, he moved his plump hands from the back of his bed to her shoulders, leaning against her and enveloping her in that sweet scent of sleepiness and warmth which only children possess, and began rubbing himself against her neck and shoulder.

"I knew!" he said, opening his eyes. "To-day is my birthday. I knew you would come!"

COUNT LEO TOLSTOY
(1828–1910) from *Anna Karenina*

Chapter Two

AND I WILL SING A LULLABY

A Cradle Song

GOLDEN slumbers kiss your eyes,
Smiles awake you when you rise.
Sleep, pretty wantons, do not cry,
And I will sing a lullaby:
Rock them, rock them, lullaby.

Care is heavy, therefore sleep you;
You are care, and care must keep you.
Sleep, pretty wantons, do not cry,
And I will sing a lullaby:
Rock them, rock them, lullaby.

THOMAS DEKKER (1572 (?) – 1632) *A Cradle Song*

IT is the nightly custom of every good mother after her children are asleep to rummage in their minds and put things straight for next morning, repacking into their proper places the many articles that have wandered during the day. If you could keep awake (but of course you can't) you would see your own mother doing this, and you would find it very interesting to watch her. It is quite like tidying up drawers. You would see her on her knees, I expect, lingering humorously over some of your contents, wondering where on earth you had picked this thing up, making discoveries sweet and not so sweet, pressing this to her cheek as if it were as nice as a kitten, and hurriedly stowing that out of sight. When you wake in the morning, the naughtiness and evil passions with which you went to bed have been folded up small and placed at the bottom of your mind; and on the top, beautifully aired, are spread out your prettier thoughts, ready for you to put on.

JM BARRIE from *Peter Pan*

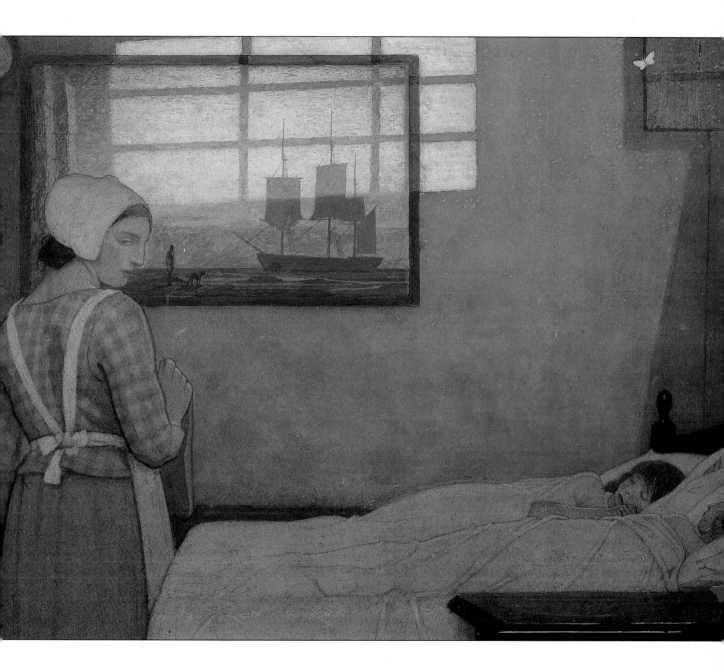

Now in memory comes my mother,
As she used, in years agone,
To regard the darling dreamers
Ere she left them till the dawn.

COATES KINNEY from *Rain On The Roof*

A Rocking Hymn

Sweet baby, sleep: what ails my dear?
  What ails my darling thus to cry?
Be still, my child, and lend thine ear,
  To hear me sing thy lullaby.
My pretty lamb, forbear to weep;
Be still, my dear; sweet baby, sleep.

GEORGE WITHER (1588 – 1667)

Lo! at the couch where infant beauty sleeps,
Her silent watch the mournful mother keeps;
She, while the lovely babe unconscious lies
Smiles on her slumbering child with pensive eyes.

CAMPBELL from *The Pleasures of Hope*

THE clocks were striking midnight, and the rooms were very still, as a figure glided quietly from bed to bed, smoothing a coverlid here, settling a pillow there, and pausing to look long and tenderly at each unconscious face, to kiss each with lips that mutely blessed, and to pray the fervent prayers which only mothers utter. As she lifted the curtain to look out into the dreary night, the moon broke suddenly from behind the clouds, and shone upon her like a bright, benignant face, which seemed to whisper in the silence: "Be comforted, dear soul! There is always light behind the clouds."

LOUISA M ALCOTT from *Little Women* first published 1868

Oor Mither –
Tribute of a Glasgow Laddie

WHEN bedtime came, each blinkin' wean
His simple verse repeated;
An' when the last his turn had ta'en
A mither's voice entreated.

Wi' he'rt upraised tae heaven abune
She'd ask the Lord tae bless us
An' syne, when we were cuddled in,
She'd gently come and kiss us.

J. DRUMMOND from *The People's Friend (Vol. XXVI)*, 1894

Published by John Leng & Co., Dundee, printers

A Cradle Song

Sweet dreams form a shade,
O'er my lovely infants head.
Sweet dreams of pleasant streams.
By happy silent moony beams.

Sweet sleep with soft down,
Weave thy brows an infant crown.
Sweet sleep Angel mild,
Hover o'er my happy child.

Sweet smiles in the night,
Hover over my delight.
Sweet smiles Mothers smiles
All the livelong night beguiles.

Sweet moans, dovelike sighs,
Chase not slumber from thy eyes.
Sweet moans, sweeter smiles.
All the dovelike moans beguiles.

Sleep sleep happy child.
All creation slept and smil'd.
Sleep sleep, happy sleep.
While o'er thee thy mother weep.

WILLIAM BLAKE (1757 – 1827)

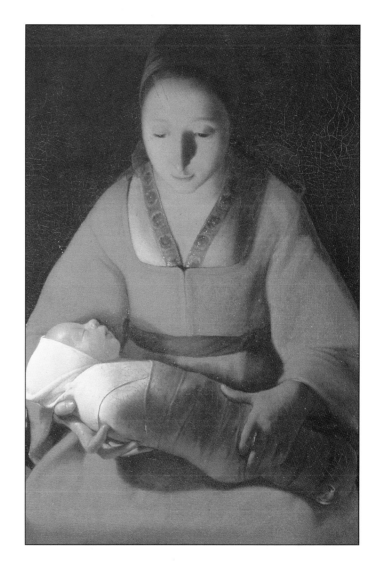

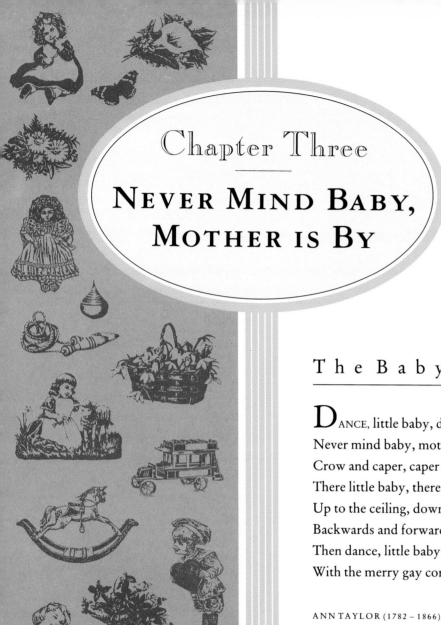

Chapter Three

NEVER MIND BABY, MOTHER IS BY

The Baby's Dance

DANCE, little baby, dance up high,
Never mind baby, mother is by;
Crow and caper, caper and crow,
There little baby, there you go:
Up to the ceiling, down to the ground,
Backwards and forwards, round and round.
Then dance, little baby, and mother shall sing,
With the merry gay coral, ding, ding, a-ding, ding.

ANN TAYLOR (1782 – 1866)

The Sick Child

CHILD   O Mother, lay your hand on my brow!
          O mother, mother, where am I now?
          Why is the room so gaunt and great?
          Why am I lying awake so late?

MOTHER   Fear not at all: the night is still.
          Nothing is here that means you ill –
          Nothing but lamps the whole town through,
          And never a child awake but you.

MOTHER   Out in the city, sounds begin.
          Thank the kind God, the carts come in!
          An hour or two more, and God is so kind,
          The day shall be blue in the window blind,
          Then shall my child go sweetly asleep,
          And dream of the birds and the hills of sheep.

ROBERT LOUIS STEVENSON (1850 – 94)

To an Infant

Ah cease thy Tears and Sobs, my little Life!
I did but snatch away the unclasped Knife:
Some safer Toy will soon arrest thine eye
And to quick Laughter change this peevish cry!
Poor Stumbler on the rocky coast of Woe,
Tutored by Pain each source of Pain to know
Alike the foodful fruit and scorching fire
Awake thy eager grasp and young desire:
Alike the Good, the Ill offend thy sight,
And rouse the stormy Sense of shrill Affright!
Untaught, yet wise! mid all thy brief alarms
Thou closely clingest to thy Mother's arms,
Nestling thy little face in that fond breast
Whose anxious Heavings lull thee to thy rest!

Man's breathing Miniature! thou mak'st me sigh –
A Babe art thou – and such a Thing am I!
To anger rapid and as soon appeased,
For trifles mourning and by trifles pleased,
Break Friendship's Mirror with a tetchy blow,
Yet snatch what coals of fire on Pleasure's altar glow!

SAMUEL TAYLOR COLERIDGE (1772–1831)

A mother does
not hear the
music of the dance
when her
children cry.

German proverb

A Lesson for Mamma

Dᴇᴀʀ Mamma, if you just could be
A tiny little girl like me,
And I your mamma, you would see
    How nice I'd be to you.
I'd always let you have your way;
I'd never frown at you and say,
    'You are behaving ill today,
    Such conduct will not do.'

I'd always give you jelly-cake
For breakfast, and I'd never shake
My head, and say, 'You must not take
    So very large a slice.'
I'd never say, 'My dear, I trust
You will not make me say you *must*
Eat up your oatmeal'; or 'The crust
    You'll find, is very nice.'

But, Mamma dear, you cannot grow
Into a little girl, you know,
And I can't be your mamma; so
    The only thing to do,
Is just for you to try and see
How very, very nice 'twould be
For *you* to do all this for *me*,
    Now, Mamma, *couldn't* you?

SYDNEY DAY (MRS COCHRA) c1881

Washing and Dressing

AH! why will my dear little girl be so cross,
  And cry, and look sulky, and pout?
To lose her sweet smile is a terrible loss,
  I can't even kiss her without.

You say you don't like to be washed and be drest,
  But would you not wish to be clean?
Come, drive that long sob from your dear little breast,
  This face is not fit to be seen.

If the water is cold, and the brush hurts your head,
  And the soap has gone into your eye,
Will the water grow warmer for all that you've said?
  And what good will it do you to cry?

It is not to tease you and hurt you, my sweet,
  But only for kindness and care,
That I wash you, and dress you, and make you look neat,
  And comb out your tanglesome hair.

I don't mind the trouble, if you would not cry,
  But pay me for all with a kiss;
That's right – take the towel and wipe your wet eye,
  I thought you'd be good after this.

ANNE TAYLOR (1782 – 1866)

MOTHER, may I go and bathe?
Yes, my darling daughter
Hang your clothes on yonder tree
But don't go near the water.

ANON, after Walter de la Mare's
The Scarecrow, 1945

A married servant of my mother's said to her once, in solemn tones, "You know, mum, children *thrive* in the dirt." Mother perceived the big principle underlying this statement, and determined that her own children should be perfectly clean once a day, and beyond that might get as dirty as they liked.

Our new surroundings were splendid for such an ideal. There was an attic at the top of the house for the boys' own, to set out their train lines, build with their bricks, and romp as they liked. There was a garden to grub in and trees to climb. I didn't want to make them nervous, and I hope it will be counted to me for righteousness that when I heard a "Hullo, Mother!" from the top branches of the fir, or saw a boy walking along the perilous edge of the garden wall, I went indoors to suffer in silence, often muttering to myself Hagar's "Let me not see the child die".

Not far away was a pond, containing minnows and stickle-backs, and one afternoon a little figure appeared slung about with every appliance for catching them and a glass jar for bringing them home. "I'm going fishing, Mother," he announced. "Won't you have your tea before you go?" I asked. "No; fishermen do not care to eat." The right spirit, I thought.

Occasionally it was one of the boys who set a problem to me, and I was not always equal to it. One day I was at the sink washing up the tea-things, when the youngest approached with, "Mother, who *is* the Holy Ghost?" I confess that I temporized: "I'm busy just now, darling, but another time . . ." He ran off contented and forgot his

MOLLY HUGHES
from *A Victorian Family*,
1870–1

difficulty. Another day the middle boy, chancing to be out with me alone, asked me what electricity was. Here I felt on surer ground, and enlarged on the subject at some length, not a little pleased at the silent attention of my audience. I was rewarded with, "Oh well, when Dad comes home I'll ask him, and he'll splain it properly."

YOU may have tangible wealth untold;
Caskets of jewels and coffers of gold.
Richer than I you can never be –
I had a mother who read to me.

STRICKLAND GILLILAN *The Reading Mother*

Don't aim to be an earthly Saint, with eyes
     fixed on a star,
Just try to be the fellow that your Mother
     thinks you are.

WILL S ADKIN from *Just Try To Be The Fellow*

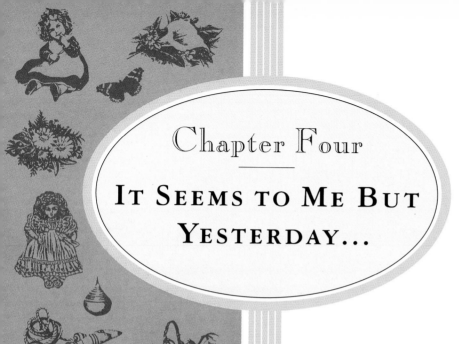

Chapter Four

It Seems to Me But Yesterday...

To Mother: A Question

THIS is the spot, my grey-grown boy,
That marks where you were born;
And that's the burn that lulled to sleep
And waked you in the morn.

Though fifty years have come and gone
And I am old and worn
It seems to me but yesterday
Since you, my boy, were born.

WILLIAM LEE from *Poems and Idyls*
Published by Dunlop and Drennan, printers,
Kilmarnock, 1907

Children

AND a woman who held a babe against her bosom said, Speak to us of Children.

And he said:

Your children are not your children.

They are the sons and daughters of Life's longing for itself.

They come through you but not from you,

And though they are with you yet they belong not to you.

You may give them your love but not your thoughts,

For they have their own thoughts.

You may house their bodies but not their souls,

For their souls dwell in the house of tomorrow, which you
cannot visit, not even in your dreams.

You may strive to be like them, but seek not to make them
like you.

For life goes not backward nor tarries with yesterday.

You are the bows from which your children as living arrows
are sent forth.

The Archer sees the mark upon the path of the infinite, and
He bends you with His might that His arrows may go
swift and far.

Let your bending in the Archer's hand be for gladness;

For even as He loves the arrow that flies, so He loves also the
bow that is stable.

KAHLIL GIBRAN (1883 – 1931) from *The Prophet*

Going into Breeches

Joy to Philip, he this day
Has his long coats cast away,
And (the childish season gone)
Puts the manly breeches on.
Officer on gay parade,
Redcoat in his first cockade,
Bridegroom in his wedding trim,
Birthday beau surpassing him,
Never did with conscious gait
Strut about in half the state,
Or the pride (yet free from sin)
Of my little manikin:
Never was there pride, or bliss,
Half so rational as his.
Sashes, frocks, to those that need 'em –
Philip's limbs have got their freedom –
He can run, or he can ride,
And do twenty things beside,
Which his petticoats forbad:
Is he not a happy lad?

CHARLES AND MARY LAMB from *Going Into Breeches* c 1870s

THE bravest battle that ever was fought;
Shall I tell you where and when?
On the maps of the world you will find it not;
It was fought by the mothers of men.

JOAQUIN MILLER *The Bravest Battle*

ALL women become like their mothers.

That is their tragedy.

No man does. That is his.

OSCAR WILDE from *The Importance of Being Earnest*

THE future destiny of the child is always
the work of the mother.

NAPOLEON BONAPARTE

The Angels are Stooping

THE angels are stooping
Above your bed.
They weary of troop,
With the whimpering dead.

God's laughing in Heaven
To see you so good;
The Sailing Seven
Are gay with His mood.

I sigh that kiss you,
For I must own
That I shall miss you
When you have grown.

WB YEATS (1865 – 1939)

AND you too, mother, you have a share in this beautiful work. For you helped me all you could in my first years, you kept me healthy and active, you strove to stimulate my mind, so that it would not be quenched in darkness and silence. How precious your motherhood is as I think what blessing you have helped to bring to mothers all over the world. Here is a treasure of comfort for you to lay up in your heart on your birthday.

With a heartful of love for you all, and with a bookful of news yet to come, I am,

Your affectionate child,
Helen Keller

HELEN KELLER in a letter to her mother, 1908
Printed courtesy American Foundation for the Blind, Helen Keller Archives

THEY say that man is mighty,
He governs land and sea,
He wields a mighty scepter
O'er lesser powers that be;
But a mightier power and stronger
Man from his throne has hurled,
For the hand that rocks the cradle
Is the hand that rules the world.

WILLIAM ROSS WALLACE from
What Rules The World c1865

Dear mother,   25 December 1854

Into your Christmas stocking I have put my 'first-born', knowing that you will accept it with all its faults (for grandmothers are always kind), and look upon it merely as an earnest of what I may yet do; for, with so much to cheer me on, I hope to pass in time from fairies and fables to men and realities.

Whatever beauty or poetry is to be found in my little book is owing to your interest in and encouragement of all my efforts from the first to the last; and if ever I do anything to be proud of, my greatest happiness will be that I can thank you for that, as I may do for all the good there is in me; and I shall be content to write if it gives you pleasure . . .

I am ever your loving daughter,

Louy

LOUISA M ALCOTT

There was a Child Went Forth

THERE was a child went forth every day,
And the first object he look'd upon, that object he
  became,
And that object became part of him for the day or a certain
  part of the day,
Or for many years or stretching cycles of years.

The early lilacs became part of this child,
And grass and white and red morning-glories, and white and
  red clover, and the song of the phœbe-bird,
And the Third-month lambs and the sow's pink-faint litter,
  and the mare's foal and the cow's calf,
And the noisy brood of the barnyard or by the mire of the
  pondside,
And the fish suspending themselves so curiously below there,
  and the beautiful curious liquid,
And the water-plants with their graceful flat heads, all
  became part of him.
His own parents, he that had father'd him and she that had
  conceiv'd him in her womb and birth'd him,
They gave this child more of themselves than that,
They gave him afterward every day, they became part of him.

WALT WHITMAN (1819 – 1892)

Youth fades; love droops; the leaves of friendship fall:
A mother's secret love outlives them all.

OW HOLMES, from *The Mother's Secret*

Acknowledgements

The publishers have made every effort to trace copyright holders. If we have inadvertantly omitted to acknowledge anyone, we should be most grateful if this could be brought to our attention.

The following pictures are reproduced with kind permission of the Bridgeman Art Library, London:

Front jacket: *The Happy Mother* by Antoine de Bruyckes (1816–84) Josef Mensing Gallery, Hamm-Rhynern. Back jacket: *Bathing (c1881)* by Mary Cassatt (1844–1926) Lauros/Giraudon. Endpapers & p1: *Playing with baby* by Adolf-Julius Berg (1820–1926) Musee du Petit-Palais/Giraudon. p2 *Sunny Hours* by Charles Lucy (1814–73) Agnew & Sons, London. p5 *Mother and Daughter*by Thomas Kennington (1856–1916) Gavin Graham Gallery, London. p7 *Motherhood, 1898* by Louis (Emile) Adan (1839–1937) Waterhouse and Dodd, London. p8 *Mother and Child with a poppy* by Frederick Richard Pickersgill (1820–1900) Roy Miles Gallery, 29 Bruton Street, London W1. p11 *The Cradle*, 1872 by Bertha Morisot (1841–95) Musee d'Orsay, Paris/Giraudon. p13 *The Coming Nelson*, from the Pears Annual, 1901 by Frederick Morgan (1856–1927) A&F Pears Ltd, London. p14 *The Adoration of the Shepherds* by Guido Reni (1575–1642) Pushkin Museum, Moscow. p16 *Mother playing with children in an interior* by Helen Allingham (1848–1926) Private Collection. p17 *The Ball of Wool by Dorothea Sharp* (1874–1955) John Davies Fine Paintings, Stow-on-the-Wold, Glos. p19 *Maternal Love* by Vicenzo Irolli (1860–1942) Josef Mensing Gallery, Hamm-Rhynern. p21 *The New Baby* by Evert Pieters (1856–1932) Private Collection. p23 *A Summer Evening* c1925 by Frederick Cayley Robinson (1862–1927) Private Collection. p25 *Mother and Baby* by Dutch School (19th century) Josef Mensing Gallery, Hamm-Rhynern. p26 *Interior of a Swiss Cottage* by J. Murray Ince (1806–59) Haworth Art Gallery, Accrington, Lancs. p27 *A Point of Interest* by Elizabeth Stanhope Forbes (1859–1912) David Messum Gallery. p28 *The end of a happy day* by Thomas Faed (1826–1900) Josef Mensing Gallery, Hamm-Rhynern. p29 *The New Born Child* by Georges de la tour (1593–1652) Musee des Beaux-Arts, Rennes. p31 *Mother and Child* by Charles James Lewis (1830–92) Christopher Wood Gallery, London. p32 *Sweet Dreams* by Thomas Brooks (1818–91) Phillips Fine Art Auctioneers. p33 *Woman with Child* by Hector Caffieri (1847–1932) Bonhams, London. p35 *Maternity*, 1921 by Achille Funi (b.1890) Private Collection London. p35 (small) *Mother and Child* by Maurice Denis (1870–1943) Hermitage, St. Petersburg/Bridgeman Art Library, London. p36 *The Sewing Lesson* by Edward Charles Barnes (fl.1856–82) Phillips, The International Fine Art Auctioneers. p37 *Couralescent* by Charles West the Younger Cope (1811–90) Christopher Wood Gallery, London. p38 *Mother and child* (pastel) by Mary Cassatt (1844–1926) Private Collection/Giraudon/Bridgeman Art Library, London. p39 *Bathing (c1881)* by Mary Cassatt (1844–1926) Lauros/Giraudon. p40/41 *The Lesson* by E. Zampighi (1859–1944) Phillips, The International Fine Art Auctioneers/Bridgeman Art Library, London. p42 *A Fairy Tale* by Carlton Alfred Smith (1853–1946) Towneley Hall Art Gallery & Museum, Burnley. p43 *The First Lesson* by Samuel Baruch Halle (1824–89) Christopher Wood Gallery, London/Bridgeman Art Library, London. p44 *Jubilee Hat* by F.W. Bourdillon (1851–1924) Private Collection. p47 *A Cottage by the Sea* by John Burr (1831–93) Beaton-Brown Fine Paintings, London. p48 *Sickness and Health*, 1843 by Thomas Webster (1800–86) Victoria & Albert Museum, London. p50 *Contentment* by Adolf Eberle (1843–1914) Josef Mensing Gallery, Hamm-Rhynern. p52 *A Great Mother* by Cesare Felix dell'Acqua (1821–1904) The Fine Art Society, London. p53 *Venetian Christening* by Henry Woods (1846–1921) Towneley Hall Art Gallery & Museum, Burnley. p54 *Baby's Birthday* by Frederick Daniel Hardy (1826–1911) Wolverhampton Art Gallery, Staffs./Bridgeman Art Library, London. p55 *"Little one who straight has come Down the Heavenly Stairs"*, 1888 by Arthur Hughes (1832–1915) Russell-Cotes Art Gallery and Museum, Bournemouth. p56 *A Mother and her Small Children* by Edith Hume (fl.1862–92) Josef Mensing Gallery, Hamm-Rhynern. p59 *Sleeping Mother*, 1883 by Christian Krohg (1852–1925) Rasmus Meyers Samlinger, Bergen. p60 *Baby's First Steps* by Emile August Pinchart (b.1842) Josef Mensing Gallery, Hamm-Rhynern. p62 *My Lady is a Widow and Childless* by Marcus Stone (1840–1921). Forbes Magazine Collection, New York. p63 *A Mother and her Daughter*, 1898 by Francesco Gimeno (1858–1927) Private Collection/Index.

The pictures on the following pages are reproduced with kind permission of the Mary Evans Picture library; p22, 24, 34, 45, 51, and 57.